MENDING THE VOW

Vol. 1

STRATEGIC PRAYERS FOR COUPLES

SEEKING VICTORY IN UNLOCKING

THE IDENTITY OF THEIR MARRIAGE.

BY

Nyjha Andrews and Vater Williams

Published by Book Writing Pioneer

Cover design by Book Writing Pioneer

ISBN: Printed in the United States

Table of Contents

Trust God in the Process!
Remember the I do's!

And not only *this*, but [with joy] let us exult in our sufferings *and* rejoice in our hardships, knowing that hardship (distress, pressure, trouble) produces patient endurance; and endurance, proven character (spiritual maturity); and proven character, hope *and* confident assurance [of eternal salvation]. Such hope [in God's promises] never disappoints *us*, because God's love has been abundantly poured out within our hearts through the Holy Spirit who was given to us." Romans 5:3-5 AMP

Father, I thank You, I honor You, and I bless Your name, for You are worthy. I thank You, God, that even in the process of trusting You, I am reminded of when I first said yes to You, Lord. When I came to know You, I was excited. I said yes! I was willing to walk where You told me to walk, pray, read Your word, and get to know You. It is not the same feeling as when I first started dating and courting my spouse and getting to know them. I was willing to trust and follow them, go to different restaurants, and try new things. The excitement was there, oh Lord, because we were on this journey together, and it was new and refreshing. But today, Lord, I am at a crossroads where the seasons have shifted, and I want to mourn this moment because I want to hold on to our yesteryears. But Father, today I have to go back to trusting You! I trusted You when a storm came, and I didn't know what to do, and my footing slipped. Help me today, Father, to trust You when my footing seems lost in my marriage. Oh Lord, help me to trust You when I do not know what to do, when I don't know what to say, and when everything I say causes an argument or friction! What do I do here, Lord?

When I am impatient, I am reminded of Romans 5:3, where You told me that tribulations worketh patience and that there is a process that needs to take place to get to hope. Could it be that I'm in a process in my marriage, and I just don't like it? Oh, help me today. You never called me to like every season that happens in my marriage and in my life, God, but one thing that has stayed consistent is You were there. So, Lord, help me to find You in good times and in every place of darkness. Help me, Lord to not let my flesh be the guiding factor, but let it be Your Spirit that leads and guides me. I understood when I said, "I do," not only did I make a vow, but I also said I would pay it and not call it a mistake. Father, not only did I say I wouldn't call it a mistake, but I put on a coat that day; I put on the coat of marriage. So, Lord, help me understand that this coat has many colors; this coat, God, has many fabrics and textures. Sometimes, it can be itchy, and sometimes, I want to take it off.

But today, I am learning and choosing not to take off anything that You have put upon me. But I want to trust You through the process of it. Trust You that my skin will learn how to endure the abrasive places, that my skin will toughen and know how to deal with the places that might tickle me. My skin will learn how to deal with the areas, my Lord, that are heavier than the lighter ones. Help me to wear this coat well. Help me, Father, to mature in the very places that You have called me to. Oh Lord, help me, I need You! I need Your help, my God. Help my mouth when I want to speak against the very things that You have called me to and that I said "I do" to, so that I may recall my coat of many colors. Father, I choose to no longer fight and buckle against Your yoke, but today, Father, I say yes! I do say yes. I do say yes. I do say yes. I have to go back to the altar when I say "I do" to the vows and say "I do" in the midst of the storm, in the midst of the tears, and in the midst of the frustration and irritation. Even in the midst of the hatred and a murderous spirit that really wants to come against the covenants of my marriage! I stand before the enemy and say, "I do." I remind him that back then, I was excited about it, and today, in the midst of how I may not feel excited about it, I still say, "I do."

I trust You! I trust You when I don't trust my spouse. I trust You when I don't trust myself. I trust You when I can't trust anyone around me due to the way they're looking at my marriage! Oh Lord, my marriage looks like a mess, but I trust You! Help me, and I trust You even when You have called me to walk through the murky waters, to scrape across the dry lands, and get a little raggedy. So that I can grow and be great in the season You have called me into. Oh, ABBA, I say, "I do." I thank You for the shifting, and I thank You for the help, the healing, and the assurance that I will get through this. I have already made it through this because Your Son died for this very moment. So I say "I do" in Jesus' Mighty Name, Amen.

For this Cause, God put us Together

J ohn 18:37 – Pilate therefore said unto him, "Art thou a king then?" Jesus answered, "Thou sayest that I am a king. To this end was I born, and for this cause came I into the world..."

Father, so many times, we find ourselves wanting to get married for many reasons (sex, companionship, loneliness, finance, etc.). Yet You have a purpose for each of us. Lord, as I focus on the things outside of purpose, I find myself wanting to give up on this marriage when my mate doesn't meet my expectations. I find myself feeling like I may have made the wrong decision. All of these things are temporary. Your word tells me that "for this light affliction is but for a moment but worketh a far exceeding weight of glory," and Your word tells us "for the sufferings of this time are not worthy to be compared to the glory which shall be revealed."

You have a purpose for marriage. Each marriage has a purpose. When we marry, we need not only to know "Is this the right mate for me?" but "What is our purpose in being together?" Now that I understand I am in this for a purpose, I won't be moved if things don't go the way I expect them to go. I will say NOPE! God put us together for a reason, and I must finish that work. Let me stay and finish what God has purposed for us. Let us focus on our purpose. Now, when the highs and lows of marriage come, we won't be moved or distracted, but we will stay focused on completing the work. Finishing what God has purposed for us in the beginning. Jesus says – "To this end was I born, and for this cause came I into the world..." In this marriage, I shall focus my attention on completing my purpose. Father, I want You to be pleased with me. Strengthen me to finish the goal. I am committed. Til Death Us Do Part.

Inspired by God

2 Timothy 3:16 Thank You, Father, for how You inspire and move through the winds, breathing in and through us. You motivate us and manipulate us to be the better versions of ourselves, to be who You have called us—the purposeful US. Father, we thank You even in how You inspire us, as it says in 2 Timothy 3:16, that all scripture is given by the inspiration of God and is profitable for doctrine, for reproof, for correction, for instruction in righteousness, that the man of God may be perfectly furnished unto all good works (verse 17).

So, Father, we thank You that You inspire us to be married to become better spouses. We are inspired by how You operate, to walk in purpose despite what the situation looks like. God, You inspire us when we can't see the next step, but we're inspired to take another step. We're inspired to turn in a different direction. We're inspired, God, that when we have a plan, You will manipulate us to do something different, and it is all for our good.

So, Father, we thank You for our marriages. We thank You, Lord, that You continue to inspire us in our marriages to be the better us and not be so focused on what it takes to make our spouse the better them. Could it be that when we're inspired to be better, to do better, to make choices like spending quality time with them instead of doing daily work that would usually be done on that day, Father, could it be that helps heal and unravel the mindset? Could it help bring deliverance in their mindset, God, who will help them turn into who You have called them to be? Because it unravels the enemy. It unravels the work of the flesh. It unravels the perverted thinking that they already have a belief in about who we are, and it shows them something different. It inspires them to look again. Father, there are many times that You said, "Look again." There are many times that You will have us look again at a situation. Once, we saw death, brittleness, brokenness, and dry places, but now we can see that there is new growth in the land that was killed. Things were knocked over, and it looked different.

New things are growing up and being rebuilt. Could this be why You inspire us? Is this not why You said even reading the same scripture will give a new understanding in a new season and a new day? Could it be because of the fact that we have been inspired to look in a different direction, to look from a different perspective? So, Father, inspire us to be the wise husbands and wives that You have called us to be. Inspire us to make a step where we're not even looking at what the outcome is going to be, but we're looking at the possibility of enjoying this moment because I'm inspired to do something different. So, Father, could it be that the moment we take a step, not overthinking it, not thinking of what the outcome is going to be, but trusting that You are the God of victory, that everything we do in You, we can't help but win? We can't help but experience a level of victory or see that it all works together for our good.

So, Lord, let us take the pressure off of marriage. Let us take the pressure off of ourselves and our spouses, and let's just be inspired. Let's just be inspired to do Your will and to do it Your way. To not think about what the outcome could be and how many steps it takes to get to the center of the Tootsie Pop. But instead, Father, let's just be inspired to take the first leg. Let's just be inspired to go and take the first step and spend the time and make the step towards our spouse and to embrace and cleave, oh God. Let's be inspired not to look at yesterday's issues. Let's be inspired to not focus on what they don't measure up to and what they are doing wrong. But, Lord, let's be inspired just to be all that You have called us to be, as we are created in Your image. We look like You, so we should talk like You. Oh God, that we could be that we will have more of the symptoms and characteristics of You the more we allow ourselves to be inspired by You and manipulated by the Holy Spirit. Help us to do something different today, to just run in the snow, to just go to embrace and hug our spouse and speak life over them— not related to what we know about them but related to what the one who inspired us says about them.

Oh Father, oh Lord, the Ancient of Days, The Great I Am. We thank You for being the inspiration for our marriages today. We thank You, Lord, that we choose to be inspired by You. We look for opportunities to stand and walk in the atmosphere and inspire our spouses and inspire those around us. Help us to perform an act that You can tell us to do, all out of inspiration. So, we breathe You in today. We breathe You into our marriage. We allow You to check us where we don't want to move because of offense. Rebuke us where it's needed. Correct us. Teach us. Equip us. Redirect us. Remind us that everything we need, we already had in the womb, that we were already fearfully and wonderfully made. So, we got this. The knitting on the inside of us was inspired by Your thoughts of us. So, thank You, Father, that You already knew us, that You already knew that we would be with our spouse. So, thank You for the inspiration for this day and every day. In Jesus' name, amen.

Birth the Vision of My Marriage

S hall I bring to the moment of birth and not give delivery?" says the Lord. "Or shall I who gives delivery shut *the womb*?" says Your God." Isaiah 66:9 amp

Abba, You are the creator of all good things. You speak, and it is so. Lord, I lift the womb of my marriage to You. Lord, I cry out for the conception of the purpose of my marriage to come forth in this season. Father, I decree that we will no longer walk in barrenness in our marriage. We will bear mighty fruit, vision, and purpose in Jesus' Name. Lord, heal the places where we have scraped against Your purpose and will for our marriage. Lord, heal my tongue of everything I've ever spoken to abort what You have called to be so. Lord, have Your way in and through our hearts that any foul or perverted place that dwells inward be removed so that new ground will be exposed. Abba, You told the husband to leave his mother and Father and to cleave to his wife. Forgive us for not allowing cleaving to You to be our anchor. Lord every place that we have felt disappointment, anger, unforgiveness, hurt, frustration, and woundedness help us to let go. Help me to let go. I choose wholeness and complete healing in my marriage. I choose to walk in victory with my spouse today, and every day of Our Lives, we choose the US. Lord, I choose to trust my spouse, and I choose to trust You. Even when it seems far-fetched or difficult, I trust Your will and Your way. I remember at the altar when we said, "I do." If You brought us this far, surely You will bring us to the delivery of the purpose and plan You have for each one of us, individually and collectively. So thank You! Thank You for the birthing season, thank You for the victory season, thank You for the love season, thank You for the cleaving and closeness like never before, in Jesus's name, amen.

Lord, is it My Responsibility to go along with My Spouse at all Costs?

Job 34:3-4: "3 For the ear trieth words, as the mouth tasteth meat. 4 Let us choose to use judgment: let us know among ourselves what is good."

Father, I give You glory, honor, and praise. You have called us to walk in wisdom and discernment. Remove the spirit of fear that sometimes operates in our lives, hindering us. Grant us boldness and courage, for You have spoken it, and it must come to pass. Your word will not return void; it will do exactly what it promises. I pray for my marriage, where one partner hinders the other from moving forward in purpose. Father, our purpose holds blessings and answers to prayers in it. Father, don't let the enemy use my mate to create hindrances and discouragement in our household. Remove fear of retribution, rejection, and retaliation from our spouses. Grant them wisdom to understand Your plan and purpose as You are impacting their spouse's life. I break the soul ties, mindsets, and root causes of hindrances. There are numerous hindrances and attacks, even from family members. I ask for the breaking and destruction of these hindrances, witchcraft, and sorcery prayers. Deliver us from evil, Jesus, and tear down the walls of hindrances and rejection, and help fulfill the purposes You've called us to.

I seek prayers that work, that transform, that bring victory and strategies in the name of Jesus. I decree a new day, a new way, purpose, and obedience in the name of Jesus Christ. I thank You for Your blessing, peace, and joy. Renew our joy, oh God. I also thank You for a heart of repentance. I bind the spirit of Pride that hinders reconciliation and humbly walk through challenges.

Father, we made a covenant and vow to each other, and our first Covenant is to You. You are our Savior and the Lord over our lives, our ruler, controller, healer, strength, and success. I thank You for Your presence, approval, acknowledgment, and validation.

I claim victory over marriages that ensure their success and longevity. Guide us, help us stand strong, and lead us in the way You want us to go. I trust You, Father. I claim unexpected victories and ask for Your guidance in every step we take. In Jesus' name, we pray for deliverance, renewal, strength, and victory. Amen.

When your Mate offends you

When your mate (he/she) offends/wrongs you, let it go as if you sinned against your own body. Ephesians 5:28 - So ought men to love their wives as their own bodies. He that loveth his wife loveth himself. Father, You told us that the two shall become one (Mark 10:8) flesh. Father, Your word tells us in Ephesians that a man should love his wife as his own body. When he loves his wife, he loveth himself. Well, today, my mate has offended me. However, when he/she offended me according to Your word, he/she offended him/herself. So today, Father, I let it go as if I sinned against myself. With us being one, when he/she offended me, it is like I offended me. So, I forgive him/her just like I would forgive myself for doing something wrong. I repent on his/her behalf today. When You deliver me (us being one), You deliver my mate. Lord, remove any areas in which I struggle to forgive myself and them so that I can stand in intercession on behalf of the US. Thank You, Father, that we are one in the spirit, and I can come to You on behalf of my mate, and as You see me, You see my mate. I truly forgive and hold no anger/unforgiveness towards my mate for that offense. I let it go. Forgiving my mate is forgiving me.

In Jesus' name, Amen!

I Forgive My Spouse; Father Forgive them

I forgive my mate! Father, forgive them, for they do not know what they do. Father, today I am disappointed because my mate (fill in the offenses). Today, I choose to forgive my mate. I choose not to hold anger towards them. That is for them as well as my mental peace. You told us that if we forgive men their trespasses, your heavenly Father will also forgive you. Matthew 6:14. To be able to remain in my marriage, I must learn to forgive every day and sometimes multiple times a day. Give me a heart that is quick to forgive and move beyond the moment of trauma/frustration. Lord, now that I have forgiven my mate, I want to ask You to forgive them. Jesus said in Luke 23:34 Father forgive them for they know not what they do. Sometimes, my mate doesn't understand when they offend the least, and they offend You. Help my mate to be aware of their impact on me/themselves. Help my mate and me so that we don't continue to repeat the same offenses towards one another. Help me to be silent so that You can speak loudly to my mate. Thank You, Father, for peace in the midst of maturing us. In Jesus' Name, Amen!

Focus on us

Phillippians 2:2-3 Then make my joy complete by being like-minded, having the same love, being one in spirit and of one mind. Do nothing out of selfish ambition or vain conceit. Rather, in humility, value others above yourselves. NIV Amos 3:3. -Do two walk together unless they have agreed to do so? NIV

Father, we struggle in our marriage to get on one accord. We struggle to focus on what is best for our marriage vs our individual desires. Lord, help us today to move past our selfish desires and focus on US. Your word tells us in Amos 3:3, "Can two walk together except they be agreed?" We choose to agree and go beyond that. Help us not just give our mate our approval, but we need to find out what is best for US. The US doesn't look like me or my mate but it looks like a combination of each of us. May our focus be on what is best for US. Let us focus on what's best for US. If we want a house, then we should deprive both of our selfish desires and get on one accord and focus on the US. As we walk together, let our goal be "What is best for US?" Thank You, Father, that in this marriage, I/we focus on the US and not just the ME. We thank You, Father, in Jesus' name, amen!

Cause Me to be a Giver In My Marriage

You shall freely and generously give to him, and your heart shall not be resentful when you give to him, because for this [generous] thing the Lord Your God will bless You in all Your work and in all Your undertakings." Deuteronomy 15:10 amp

Father, we bless and glorify You. You are so worthy. What a mighty God You are, and we honor You today, God, because You are a God of order. You go before us and make the crooked places straight, so the path is always clear before us if we follow You and apply the knowledge that You have given us to be wise. So, God, we thank You for the wisdom and how to put things in order. If You are a God who has a plan, then You expect us to have a plan. If You are a God with a blueprint, You expect us to have a blueprint. You prepare us for what-ifs. So, Father, we pray for our marriage to come on one accord. We bind up the spirit of division and pray against the lack of communication that hinders couples from doing what they need to do. Father, we speak to the body of believers. We thank You, Father, that You prepare us to be upgraded and open up our mindsets and hearts being upgraded to where You have called us to be givers. Father, You said that giving is like a cycle; it's a circle, and if everyone is giving, everyone is also receiving. Father, You said that

You created this because Your son was the best giver even through the work of the cross. It had to continue to move, so giving is a movement.

Lord, we thank You that You open us to be givers. You open us, God, to receive and not be envious of what one gives and what one receives, knowing that if it's a cycle, we all have more than enough, and every need is met. Lord, open our hearts to break the bondage and ties of religion, selfishness, lack, poverty mindsets, and trauma from past lives that stand in the way of our victory, that stand in the way of the very things that You have called us to. Father, help us that we will no longer stand in our own way and resist giving. Instill in us a heart of giving, enhancing, and upgrading one another without worrying about ourselves.

You said that You will perfect the things that concern us. If I'm so concerned about myself that it hinders my giving. I'm standing in Your way to perfect me, to perfect what giving looks like unto me. Lord, teach us to let our hands go and be the body and not just try to preserve ourselves. But this is how we preserve and heal the body; this is how we operate and show the manifestation of Your goodness.

So, Lord, we thank You that You continue to have Your way in and through us. Father, I thank You for removing the hindrances. We thank You, Lord, for removing/crushing everything that stands in the way of victory, everything, God, even fear of what happens if they keep moving up or what happens when we keep asking questions and keep seeking more of You, Father. Help us that we keep expanding. Our capacity will keep growing, so let us stay open to the capacity shift. Let us stay open to the liberty and freedom that You give us. Let us give... it's not okay to hold back what You have given us to share. It's not okay to stand in the way of those who are called to what You have given us for them. It's not okay to cause strife and let bitterness or your own bondage be a stumbling block for the cycle that the Lord has already created.

So, help us to get in a position to give away what God provided in us for others. Let us step out of the way so others can give us what God has provided for us through them. We honor You and bless You in Jesus' name. Amen.

Raise up Laborers that will Minister to Married Couples

Mathew 9:37: The harvest truly is ripe, but the laborers are few. Father, You have provided for all Your children to be ministered to. You said You set in the church Apostles, Evangelist, Pastors, Prophets, and Teachers for the perfecting of the saints. Truly, Father, Your married couples need to be perfected. Thank You, Father, for raising up laborers who will minister to married couples so that they will be able to be fruitful and be sustained through challenges that may arise. Also, Father, remind us that help is needed, not just when things are going bad. They need to be able to mature enough in their marriages and understand how to be successful, raise their children, handle their finances, household management etc. How do we work through situations when we both feel we are right and giving in feels like I lost something? Lord, we need laborers to help us to tunnel through the differences that make us who we are, yet You have called us to be one. Father thank You for those that You have called to pray for our marriages. You said in Your word they shall bring forth fruit in his season Psalm 1:3. May they seek Your face for the needs of Your people collectively and individually. May they bow their knees to You Ephesians 3:14 in prayer that Your married couples will be victorious and not give up. Oh, Father only You would be mindful of husbands and wives that You would call someone to pray just for them. May those who are called obey You and move into their calling. For when they obey You, it supplieth the want of the saints, but is abundant also by many thanksgivings unto God; whiles by the experiment of this ministration they glorify God for Your professed subjection unto the gospel of Christ, and for Your liberal distribution of them and unto all men. Thanks be unto God for His unspeakable gift to us all. 2 Corinthians 9:12-15.

Do Something for your Mate Just to Please them

Luke 6:35 b-36 NIV – Lend to our enemies without expecting not get anything back. Then your reward will be great, and you will be children of the Most High, because he is kind to the ungrateful and wicked. Be merciful, just as your Father is merciful.

Lord, cleanse my heart today. You are moving on my heart to do something for my mate not expecting anything in return. Lord, I choose to forgive my mate and release them from any offense they may have done against me. Lord, move my desires and motives out of the way. Let me focus on my mate. Lord, give me an idea that would make them happy. Give me an idea that they would take pleasure in. Let my joy be in their happiness. Even if they don't say thank you, if they don't appreciate what we did if they don't tell others of this thing that was done for them, I will take pleasure in knowing that I am the child of the Most High because You are kind to the ungrateful. Father, let me be merciful just as You are merciful.

In Jesus' name, we pray, amen!

Help us see things clearly when we see with dim, Hurt Shields Upon Our Hearts

1 Corinthians 13:12 For now we see through a glass, darkly; but then face to face: now I know in part; but then shall I know ever as also I am known.

Heavenly Father, the greatest communicator, the clearest visionary that we will ever know in our lives, we adore You, Lord. We thank You for Your goodness and Your mercy. Thank You, God, that when You created us, You gave us so much inside. You gave us all these senses and abilities to communicate, not even just with our words, but with the way we touch, the way we feel, and the way we come into a room. Lord, people can pick up on how we feel just with our vibes. But what is that really? It's our spirit. It's really how we present ourselves and how we view ourselves in You.

So, Lord, when we see through a dim shield, is it how we see ourselves, too? It hinders how we view others. It hinders how all things seem to not work together for us and how we struggle with situations and outcomes because of the dim light in the mirror that we're looking through. Because of our own wounds, everything spoken seems to hurt, wounds, and sometimes humiliates us. It abuses and offends us. As children, we take on views from watching our parents. Lord, expose those dimly lit views that need to be transformed. We submit to Your vision and lay down the unGodly patterns of our parents. Let us say, "I refuse to look through lights and see such a dim place."

Help us today, Father, that even as we want to operate from I Corinthians 13, God, You said, for now, in this time of imperfection, we see in the mirror dimly, a blurred reflection, a riddle, an enigma. But then, here's the 'but.' God, You always provide a way out. You always provide the bridge. But then, when the time of perfection comes, we will see reality face to face. Now, I know in part, just in fragments, but then I will know fully just as I have been fully known by God. But when is the 'but' then, Father? You said that if we continue to align with the fullness that You planned for us when You knitted us in our mother's womb, making us fearfully, wonderfully made, You said our soul knows it well. Our soul is already aware of all that we are. Everything that we need to be equipped with was already knitted in us at the beginning when it was You and wisdom on the earth. You saw void, and You spoke about what it was going to look like, and You started to speak. It was You and wisdom, and then You created the earth and created all that was in it.

So, Lord, now we stand before You with our dim lights of issues from our past and our histories, and we say, speak unto us. Let Your voice continue to speak upon us. Speak upon every dim place in the mirror that we still look through where our spouses don't appear in the best view because we still hear the hurt of our childhood. We still hear the hurt of our own and their past yesterday. Oh, Father, we thank You that You still give us another chance to get it right. You still give us another chance to stay married. You still do in the land of the living because the moment we die, the marriage is over. The moment we die to our natural or even die to ourselves, something shifts. The moment we give into our flesh, we divorce. The moment we give in to the accuser, it's done.

But today, Father, we go after the very places that the accuser plays on. He plays on making sure that the dim mirror is clean and ready for us to see everything in it. We look at our spouses and see the hurt places that they bring and that they poke at. This gives us insight into where to poke and where to touch. It shows how to use the children, how to use our wounded places—those we cry unto You about and use that against us. And then we look at them and say, "Oh, nothing good can surely come from Your mouth." But today, we go after the dim places. Today, we throw rocks, not at each other, Father, but after mirrors and break the dim mirrors.

Today, God, we're looking for the full reflection. Today, we want to see You fully. We're tired of looking in the mirror and seeing through a dim mirror, looking back at ourselves and seeing how we are not enough, how we're inadequate, how we have to. Help us, Father, for we don't understand, and we can't understand the fullness there is without You. But we know that there is a dim place, and the enemy has full access to this mirror. He uses it to his advantage to kill, steal, and destroy our marriage, destroy our vision, destroy our character before each other, and how we view each other and how we view ourselves.

But today, Your light is shining. We're choosing to walk in it, Father. You said that we have to come unto You to get the fullness thereof and that we have to wait for the day of perfection. But I believe that if we come into the light, we will see all that the light has. So, Father, we step in, and we create a place where we can stand united in our marriages as Us. We can stand and give our best intentions. We can stand on You and stand in a place, Lord, that the knitting stands stronger than the accuser, that the knitting and the cleaving stand stronger, has more weight than the dim mirror. Oh, help us today. Help us today to choose to stand strong in You, to do and be all that You have called us to be because of Your love for us. For what You have knitted us and said we were fearfully and wonderfully made.

But yet, Father, we walk in fear and we wonder what fear is going to operate next in our marriage, what issue is coming next. But that is not what Your word said. You said we were fearfully and wonderfully made. So let us choose to be what the enemy fears after, the glory and the wonder that's on the inside of us. With this, we can create new things and we can speak into the atmosphere and shift the whole thing. So we're calling for a shifting of our marriage from the dim mirrored places of smoky rooms to clear places where we don't stumble and hit our feet every time we come near each other. But instead, God, we can see one another and not be ashamed. Oh, help us today. I know that You tell us to be aware of who we're coming around. You tell us to be aware and be gentle as doves. But why is it a serpent, God? I'm going after that place. I'm calling for marriages that operate in the vision that You had, and that's in unity, that says, "One, do I choose to keep things from myself?" But yet, we have to keep things from another person that You knitted us together.

I'm going after that place because I don't think that the world should have a say, nor should our flesh impact what You have called and created in heaven. You created a vision for marriage, and yet that is not what we're operating in, and it's not okay that we have to accept it and find creative and witty ways to get around it. It's not acceptable that we can't bear our whole selves because our spouses will come for us and will stab us and throw stones at us. It's not acceptable when we serve a God who said, "You have the heart of man in Your hand, so deal with the hearts and the dim places."

So I do cry for marriage just because it's not acceptable. This is not what You are. This is not what wholeness looks like. And I'm tired of settling. I'm tired of us compromising. I know it wasn't always meant to be easy, but surely having a purpose means that we're getting closer to Your perfection. Why seek something if I'm never going to get closer to You? If the US would never get closer to the vision that You created, I want to see it on this earth. I need to see an example on this earth of what Your marriage looks like in heaven. You said we can call those things down from heaven and say, "Here." So, we're calling it into the Earth Realm. Why call me a creator, a carpenter, if I can't have access to this and create what You have for us from heaven to earth? Have Your Way. Help us in whatever unbelief place, whatever fantasy place that tries to say, "Oh, that's just the fantasy. That's not the reality." But I serve a God who is so compassionate and loving and kind in all his ways, and even when he comes for us, this is why vengeance is Yours because it doesn't look like what we already imagine vengeance to look like. So show us. Manifest Your marriage in and through us.

In Jesus' name, amen.

Lord Give Me the Ministry of Silence: Lord, Help Us

COMMUNICATE EFFECTIVELY

Lord, help my mate and me learn to communicate effectively. When we disagree, we sometimes argue as the way to solve problems. It takes two people to argue. But, if I hold my tongue, You will fight that battle for the US. You told us that our conversation can win our mate including holding my words. Because of our reverence for You, arguing with my mate is arguing in Your presence. 1 Peter 3:1-2. May we have reverential fear for You, Father. May we allow You to strengthen our communication. May we allow You to help us to communicate in a way that doesn't tear each other down but resolves and addresses matters that need to be worked out. May we never put each other down. May we never say hateful things about each other or each other's families. May we always look to build each other up. May we always find ways to say things in a way that is truthful but not hurtful.

Thank You, Father, for helping us to communicate. May we learn to keep our tongue from speaking things that are not true. May we learn to listen to understand and not pause just to jump back in and get our point across. Oh Lord, help us. Sometimes, it isn't necessary to make a point. Help us to discern when to just keep our thoughts to ourselves and focus on our mate. LORD HELP US BOTH.

Ministry of Silence: You Are Calling Me to Shut My Mouth

The Lord will fight for you while you [only need to] keep silent and remain calm."-Exodus 14:14

"Ye shall not fear them: for the Lord your God he shall fight for you." - Deuteronomy 3:22

"In the same way, you wives, be [a]submissive to your own husbands [subordinate, not as inferior, but out of respect for the responsibilities entrusted to husbands and their accountability to God, and so partnering with them] so that even if some do not obey the word [of God], they may be won over [to Christ] without discussion by the godly lives of their wives," -1 Peter 3:1

Father, today I find myself speaking when I sense You want me to be silent. There are times when I know what I said created a rift in my marriage, and I regret my words. There are times when I should be listening, yet–I am busy talking. Lord, You have so many scriptures that encourage us to be still/quiet, etc., and let You fight the battle, yet we don't. Today, I ask for Your help to be silent. I need Your help in shutting my mouth. I ask for Your help to respect my mate when they are talking. Not just to pause but to listen. I don't always have to have something to say. I don't have to defend myself.

I don't always have to convince my mates that I am right and they are wrong. It is okay that I don't "win" the conversation.

What is important is that the "US" wins. Sometimes, it must be enough that You, Father, know who is right and who is wrong. You promised in Your word that YOU will fight for me. Father, fight this battle for "US." Deliver us. I will shut my mouth. I don't have to have the last say. It is okay that my mate thinks they won the argument. I want You to get the glory. I want to have a victorious marriage. If that means me shutting my mouth, then so it be. Father, Your word says that we can win our mate over without words but by our behavior. Thank You, Lord, for Total victory over my mouth.

It is in Jesus' Name I pray AMEN!!

I am not in the Mood!

Your word says in Song of Solomon 3:1-4 "By Night on my bed I saw him who my soul loveth, I sought him but I found him not I will rise now and go about the city and the streets and then the broad ways I will seek Him whom my soul loveth I sought him but I found him not. The watchman that go about the city found me. To whom I said: Saw ye him who my soul loveth It was but a little that I passed from them but I found him whom my soul loveth. I held him and would not let him go…"

In the name of Jesus, Father, I pray for the areas of intimacy that we are struggling in. Oh Father, there are times when one of us is thinking about the other mate all day long. Sometimes, Father, the focus is so much on their name, rejecting those advances. We misunderstand, Father, that those advances are what You give as a natural ability for husbands and wives to desire each other. Husbands and wives should think about each other's bodies, draw them together, oh God. Yet, there are times when one mate may not reciprocate. They may misinterpret that advance as constantly wanting them to be sexual. But Father, You give us an internal emotional mechanism on the inside, Father, that causes us to long for our mate, that causes us to desire our mate, that causes us to think about them, to be drawn to them, Father.

Help us, Father, to reciprocate their desires... Help us, Hallelujah, to receive and not cause our mate to turn off their desire, Father. Oh Lord, thank You today, Father, that You deal with us in the area of intimacy, help us to be intimate with each other even when we don't feel like it. It's not necessarily always a sexual encounter, God, but maybe it's the intimacy of rubbing, maybe it's the intimacy of cuddling, a kiss, oh God, maybe it's just intimacy. But Lord God, You give us this emotion, Father, to desire our own mate. Let us not reject that desire. Let us not reject our mate. Let us not try by any means to turn off God what You've given to draw us together.

As Exodus 20:17 let us not covet another's mate however, let us desire our mate. Exhaust any flames that have ignited toward anyone else. Heal my rejected places so my mind can mature and be transformed to handle the longing, the communication, the comforting, and all forms of intimacy that tighten the fibers of our marriage. Lord, I need rooted perseverance to endure the longing of my mate like You long for my worship.

Father God, let us give in to that fire, give in to that desire, give in to that thing that draws us together, give into that thing that we long for, that is drawing us into longing for our mate throughout the day. The longing that causes us to think, "I can't wait to tell my husband this. I can't wait to tell my wife that. I can't wait to hold her hand. I can't wait to give him a kiss." The book of Songs of Solomon says She longed for him, and she woke up, and he was not there. So, she went in the streets and began to inquire about where he was until she found him because her desire was for her own mate, not just anybody, oh God. Let us be reminded of that. Let us not reject our mate. Let us not send them out to seek somebody else. But let us comfort and accept them. Thank You, Father, for healing our emotions.

Thank You, Father, for transforming my thinking. Thank You, Father, for helping me to see those areas in which I do not understand why my mate is desiring me at this moment. Help me to be patient and resist my own self when I want to fight against the desires of my spouse as they chase after me. Lord, thank You that the innermost part of me desires my mate with such a passion and such a seek that it will not only be sexual. But it's just the connecting and the cleaving of connecting and longing for our own selves, for our own identity, for our own love of self, Father. Let us love our spouse like we love ourselves. Even Your word tells us to do such a thing. Lord, we thank You that we will no longer look at them and be afflicted and offended by the past hurts. But instead, let a fire be ignited on the inside of us that we long to go after them, to seek after them like You seek after us. We long to be connected in one with them, the way You long to connect and be one with us, oh Lord.

We want to long after our spouses and be so concerned about their whereabouts that we will go in the streets, the highways, and byways and look for them. The same way that You go when You're concerned and You seek after us. And You say, "Where are You, Lord?" even knowing where we are, but being that we are now so concerned with them that when we embrace them, we no longer think of the past hurt. But we think of what the future at this moment will have for us. Let this be a healing place. Let this be a place that we can now be rooted in. This is our new healing place. This is a new foundation and a new grounding for us. Plant us so that we can be connected in the ground together. Connect us. Make us one again. Stir a desire, Father, that stirs our intimate spots that it stirs us, Lord, and let our flesh connect with our spirit and our mind. Then now we can actually experience what one really is with our spouse, oh Lord.

Help us today that this will be a place, a new anchored spot. So, when the next issue, the next storm, comes, we can try to come back and be reminded of where we were once anchored and once grounded. So, let us find ourselves thinking of the good things about our spouse, thinking of them, reading the Song of Solomon and putting our spouse's name in there, calling them, sending text messages, and having quick rendezvous with our spouse. Because that's Your desire for us, to love our spouse, to want them, to desire them, to connect with them. How can we say we want purpose if we don't even know how to really connect with the very thing we are purposed with?

So, Father, we thank You for the stirring. We thank You for the fire. We thank You for igniting us to be each other's catalysts, to cultivate the ground, and to stir into the places that we thought were settled. But now we have chosen to turn over the soil of our desire for each other, oh Lord. We thank You. We honor You and bless You, and we thank You, God, that we choose to rock their world as much as they want to rock ours.

In Jesus' name, amen.

Lord, Deliver Me From Self Pity

For Your servants find [melancholy] pleasure in the stones [of her ruins] And feel pity for her dust." Psalms 102:14

Father, thank You for loving us and being patient with us. Lord, I come to You on behalf of our marriage. Father, we thank You for helping us overcome our own pitiful places. Sometimes, Lord, I find pleasure in sorrow, seeking sympathy and hoping my spouse will rescue me. Today, Lord, I thank You that I no longer seek pleasure in my sorrow. Instead, I choose to rise from this place and find victory in every step towards our marriage.

Lord, I repent for seeking something from my spouse that only You can provide because You are a great provider. Everything I need comes from You. Thank You, Lord, for healthy expectations, desires, and standards in our marriage. Thank You for the shift and renewal of my mindset when I anticipate my spouse's response. I no longer play the victim; instead, we are one and victorious in all our ways.

Father, I will no longer dwell in ruined places. I choose to rise, move past my wounds, and forgive. Thank You, Lord, that I am healed and whole. Our unity is strong in You, ABBA. I love You, and I love my mate in the mighty name of Jesus. I give You all the honor and glory. I declare that all my pitiful places are dried up! In Jesus' name, I pray. Amen.

When your Mate is Making Foolish choices that are Detrimental to the Family, Household, Finances, etc. Be the Stronger. Be the wiser.

Your word says…I Samuel 25:18 Then Abigail made haste, and took two hundred loaves, and two bottles of wine, and five sheep ready dressed, and five measures of parched corn, and an hundred clusters of raisins, and two hundred cakes of figs, and laid them on asses. 19 And she said unto her servants, Go on before me; behold, I come after You. But she told not her husband Nabal. 20 And it was so, as she rode on the ass, that she came down by the covert on the hill, and, behold, David and his men came down against her; and she met them.21 Now David had said, Surely in vain have I kept all that this fellow hath in the wilderness, so that nothing was missed of all that pertained unto him: and he hath requited me evil for good. 22 So and more also do God unto the enemies of David, if I leave of all that pertain to him by the morning light any that pisseth against the wall.

23 And when Abigail saw David, she hasted, and lighted off the ass, and fell before David on her face, and bowed herself to the ground, 24 And fell at his feet, and said, Upon me, my Lord, upon

me let this iniquity be: and let thine handmaid, I pray thee, speak in thine audience, and hear the words of thine handmaid.

Lord, today, my mate is making decisions that are not wise. You have instructed us to go another way, yet (she/he) they are not moving in that direction. Lord, I pray for wisdom in how to handle this situation. Father, cause me to hold my tongue and not argue (Psalm 141:3). I don't have to argue/debate/remind my mate of their choices and the impact. You gave me the wisdom to address the situation and save our family, household, finances, marriage, etc. Thank You, Father. You said if a man lacks wisdom to ask of You Who give liberally and withhold not (James 1:5). Thank You, Father, for wisdom. Give me the courage to step out in faith, trusting that my family will be saved. We will praise You and give You all the glory in Jesus' name, AMEN.

Lord, I Need Forgiveness

Father God today we pray the prayer of forgiveness. Father, I need forgiveness. Father, there are things that I've done in my marriage that transgressed my vow, causing my mate to be angry with me. I need forgiveness, Lord! I need Your grace, Father God, and You to look upon me. Even when Jesus was on the cross, and one of the men said Grant me to be with You in Paradise, and You said, surely this day You should be with Me and Lord God. You gave him a chance before it was over to get it right, and this is my chance. There are times, Lord, when we need the heart of our mate to be softened, to give grace, to give us another opportunity to get it right. I pray, oh Lord, that You will soften the heart of my mate. I need forgiveness! I caused this resistance in our marriage, Lord. I created this situation. Help me, Lord, to forgive myself! Even Judas felt repentance once he realized what he had done.

You told me in 1 John 1:9 that "If we confess our sins, he is faithful and just to forgive us our sins and to cleanse us from all unrighteousness." You commanded me to sin no more and turn from my wicked ways, oh Lord. You promised that when I repent, You will heal my land. Heal our land, Father God, heal our marriage, Father God. Give me another opportunity to get it right with my mate, oh Lord. Help me, Lord. I feel like I can't forgive myself for the hurt, destruction, shame, division, and affliction I have caused and brought upon my household.

I need forgiveness! You told me not to do it, but I didn't listen. I need an opportunity, an open door, a chance so I can get it right this time, in the name of Jesus. Father, shut the door on anything that I have opened to me, my family, and the generations to come that doesn't bring You glory and is not in Your will for our lives and purpose. Shut the doors to the enemy! I repent for my sins and transgressions. Let me be the one who will bring You honor, glory, peace, and joy in how I handle my mate. Thank You, Lord, for another opportunity to get it right. Thank You for your grace and mercy. Thank You, Lord for touching the heart of my mate to give me another opportunity. Thank You, Lord, for helping my mate to receive my love, respect, and honor towards them and my marriage. It is in Jesus' name I pray, Amen.

I am Angry and want to Leave

Psalm 4:3-5 "The Lord will hear when I call unto him. Stand in awe, and sin not; commune with Your own heart upon Your bed and be still. Offer the sacrifices of righteousness and put Your trust in the Lord."

Lord, who can I call and tell this to? Lord, I have a secret, and I need to tell You. Thank You that You are my Father. You already know what is in my heart, and therefore, You can hear the good and the bad. So Father, "I WANT TO LEAVE THIS MARRIAGE!" I am angry, and I feel that I can't take it anymore. Thank You, Father that I can be honest with You and tell You all about how I feel. Your word says I can commune with You in my heart upon my bed. It also says to put my trust in You. So I put my trust in You. Help me, Lord to put my focus on what is important. Help me to get past this moment of frustration/trauma and forgive my mate. I will confess with my mouth, "I CHOOSE TO FORGIVE." You have required us to forgive. So I forgive my mate.

Thank You, Father, for helping me to forgive. Thank You, Father, for helping me to move past this moment of anger, frustration, and disappointment and not give up on the whole marriage.

It is in Jesus' name I pray, Amen.

I need to tell my mate something difficult

James 1:5 – "If any of you lack wisdom, let him ask of God, that giveth to all men liberally, and upbraideth not; and it I shall be given him."

Father, today I need to share some difficult news with my mate. However, in the past, when I shared this type of information with my mate, it did not go well. I don't know if it is the way I said it or how my mate interprets this information. However, I need to tell my mate. Father, I need Your wisdom today. Holy Spirit, the word tells us in John 14:26. You shall teach us all things. I need Your direction on how to share so that we can work together and work through this situation. Be it Finances, Health, Children, Work, etc, we can resolve anything. Thank You in advance for Your guidance today. Thank You for giving me the wisdom today. I am so glad that You know my mate and me better than we know ourselves. Help us to work through the difficult conversations so that we may grow together and learn to communicate effectively.

In Jesus' Name, amen!

Temperature check! What voice are you hearing?

Your word says… "Casting down imaginations, and every high thing that exalteth itself against the knowledge of God, and bringing into captivity every thought to the obedience of Christ;"- 2 Corinthians 10:5 KJV Father we thank You we honor You and we just love You. We love the voice that You use to draw us in and how You've continued to mature it. We know Your voice and a stranger we will not follow.

Father, in our marriages, some voices and situations arise that lead us to action. We need to know if we are going in the right direction and if we are in Obedience to Christ? So Father, today we are doing like 2 Corinthians 10:5 tells us, we're "casting down imaginations and every High thing that exalts itself against the knowledge of God and bringing into captivity every thought to The Obedience of Christ."

Father, we take every thought and every voice that we hear about our marriages and advise us on how to respond to situations in our marriage. And we cast it back to Your obedience! We choose to love and no longer be moved by the voices that speak innocently through us pertaining to our feelings of anger, rage, disappointment, or even trauma. But now we command them to be subject to You. Father, we thank You that even Eli taught Samuel how to acknowledge The Voice and to know that it was not his voice. We use that same tool. We use the same wisdom and now acknowledge that the voice we heard could have been past marriages, past situations, and things that we've seen through our lineage. But today, Lord, we fall under the lineage of Christ, so we choose to allow Christ's voice to speak for our marriages.

Speak through our marriages and speak to our marriages. Oh, help us today, Father, because Pride isn't going to be like this, and the lack of compassion is going to fight us. But we choose to fight for the vision that You gave us when You birthed our marriage through us at the altar. We made a vow and said we will not call this a mistake, so Lord we choose to let every action be a payment towards the vow. Oh, help us today that we will pay our due and not walk away and not allow You to say our voice is no longer good to You. Father, we love You, we adore You, and we thank You for new wisdom and the voice of You and how You speak for our marriage. So it's in Jesus' name that we give You all the honor, and we choose to listen on. Amen

Allow My Spouse to be who they are called to become without Hindrance

James 1: 4-8 Romans 5: 3-5. Psalm 40:1 CSB and Psalm 40:8 CSB: "I waited patiently for the Lord, and he turned to me and heard my cry for help." "I delight to do Your will, my God, and Your instruction is deep within me.

ABBA, I thank You for Your goodness, mercy, and patience toward Your children. You are patient as we grow and mature. I appreciate Your perfect will being manifested before me, even when I struggle to release my own will and desires. Oh Lord, today, I choose to let go of my desires and expectations and wait patiently for Your move. Father, as I shatter the standards that I have set, created from my deficits, trauma, and fantasies. I put on Your garments of wholeness, healing, and being enough so that my vision has no choice but to shift. I will no longer measure my spouse based on my own standards, but I will set my eyes back on You; You are the standard.

Help me, oh Lord. It's not easy releasing all control of the plans that I have in place. But I hear Your inspired words refreshing me, "Many are the plans in the mind of a man, but it is the purpose of the Lord that will stand," Proverbs 19:21. I choose to stand! I stand barefoot, I stand on solid ground, I stand in Your love. When I cry, You hear me; You don't hesitate to show Yourself to me, so I will not hesitate to be present in my marriage. I delight to do Your will, my God, and Your instruction is deep within me. Here I am, patiently waiting for Your directions on my next step.

As I stand here, I choose to love my mate. Forgive me for not recognizing the complete spouse You created for me. I repent for not giving my spouse a chance to continue developing in Your glory. I required calculated actions from my spouse because I thought that was the only way to live happily ever after. But now I know the victory was already in our "Yes!" So, Abba, come upon "US" and hear the cry of our YES! I choose to walk in the steps that You ordered. Thank You for healing our land. Thank You for shifting my mindset about my mate. Thank You for the victory through our YES, in Jesus' Name. Amen.

Who am I Married to?

In the same way, you husbands, live with your wives in an understanding way [with great gentleness and tact, and with an intelligent regard for the marriage relationship], as with [a]someone physically weaker, since she is a woman. Show her honor and respect as a fellow heir of the grace of life, so that your prayers will not be hindered or ineffective."1 Peter 3:7

Lord, I struggle to get along with my mate sometimes. Just when I think I know (him/her) them, I find myself not connecting with them. Your word tells me to "dwell with them according to knowledge." Help me to know my mate. Help me to understand how to communicate with them in a collaborative way. Help me to understand how to serve them. Help me to know when to talk and when to listen. Help me to hold my tongue and truly hear my mate. Then Father, help me to interpret what I hear to what they need. (James 1:5). Truly You, Father, created my mate. You know who they are. You know what they have gone through. You know the trauma that they have experienced that has shaped their view, understanding, fears, concerns, etc. Oh, Father, only You know the (Psalm 44:21) secrets of their (his/her) heart. Let me be an answer to victory for my mate. However, I need You to show me the way to love them. Serve them. Take care of them even when they are asking for something that is the opposite of what they need. Give me the courage to be a tool that helps them become who YOU created them to be. Give me the patience to see it through. I thank You for the victory in knowing and understanding who my mate is in Jesus' Name, amen!!!

Purpose of your Union

He has saved us and called us to a holy life—not because of anything we have done but because of his own purpose and grace. This grace was given us in Christ Jesus before the beginning of time, 10 but it has now been revealed through the appearing of our Savior, Christ Jesus, who has destroyed death and has brought life and immortality to light through the gospel." II Timothy 1:9-10.

Father, what is the purpose of this marriage? What is the purpose of this union? Father, You have called this marriage/union with a holy calling before the world began. It isn't called according to our lists. It isn't according to what someone told us marriage is about. It is a holy calling from heaven. It is a calling according to Your purpose. Tell us what that purpose is. Help us to understand what that purpose is. Let us renew our minds (Romans 12:2) so that we can understand and focus our efforts according to Your purpose.

Along with that purpose, it brings life and abolishes death. This marriage will succeed if we focus on Your purpose. Father forgive me for not focusing on purpose. Deliver me from my selfishness and help me to redirect my vision/ideas/efforts to accomplish Your will. Thank You, Father, for victory! Thank You, Father, for purpose! In Jesus' name, amen!

We have Trespassed Against Our Marriage

Father, You said that we trespassed against our marriage so I put this prayer at Your feet. I put the definition of trespassing as entering to commit an offense against a person or a set of rules at Your feet. Father, I can't help but think and believe that You are saying that we have committed an offense against one another and against Your rules of marriage. You've asked us to come before You to repent, but at this moment, Lord, we are not acting or operating in an Oneness because we are in a state of trespass and distress. So, Lord, I come before You, and I repent for all that I have done, said, and even thought against my spouse and my marriage. I ask You to forgive me for making a vow before You when I said "I do" and calling it a mistake every time we have a disagreement. We continue to go before You and make sounds of war and distress as we cause ruins and set off bombs with our tongues to further cause an offense against us in the courts of heaven.

So Lord, help me to undo this trespass, help me to make right the very things that I have made wrong through my words and my actions. Don't let this flesh be a barrier and the ripper that keeps me from what You have called me to do. Lord, I fear how You held David to the standard when he trespassed against the marriage of

Uriah and Bathsheba. Father, I don't want our marriage to experience a loss of vision, purpose, or plan through death because of any trespasses that we have spoken or done. As I stand before You, I Repent on behalf of my spouse because Your word says in Matthew 19:6, "So they are no longer two, but one flesh. Therefore, what God has joined together, let no one separate." Yet it is us who continue to put each other down and cause separation.

So I stand before You as a representation of the Oneness of our marriage, and I repent for going railing for railing. I stand before You as a United marriage, and I repent for division. I stand before You, God as Your child, and repent for getting in the way of Your vision for our marriage. You have cleaved our hearts together, yet we fight the very thing that ties us together, so surely we have not just trespassed our marriage, but we have trespassed against Your will, Your way, and even the Covenant we made with You. Forgive us, for we did not know what the impact would be. We only knew how quickly we could make a comeback! Touch our lips with Your coal, heal our hearts from these ruins, and reunite us in Jesus' Name.

Lord, we're asking for You to continue to heal us so that we will no longer continue to let this be our pattern. Let us make good choices, make better choices, and find better ways in and through difficult moments. Mature us in our mindsets, our emotions, and in our tongue so that we will be slow to speak, slow to anger, but quick to hear what You're saying, our God. Heal us, strengthen us, and renew our mindset that we won't step on unlawful grounds against our marriage by disrespecting and dishonoring each other with our words or actions. Thank You for the love and patience that brings so much grace and mercy even when we have done the wrong. Thank You, Father that we can lay out before You and say we're sorry and receive a clean slate due to the blood of Jesus. Thank You, Lord we are now speaking love and kindness that You have called us to. We are now encouraging and building and birthing great Visions that You have called us to. In Jesus' name, I pray, Amen.

Speak the word in Faith Regardless of what you see. Call it what it is!

Hebrews 11:1, 3KJV, 2 John 1:8 NIV Father sometimes, I/we struggle to see success in my marriage. Sometimes I see failure, lack, divorce, etc. Yet Father, You called our marriage victorious. You called our marriage a success. So today, Father, I/we choose to take on the mind of Christ (Philippians 2:5) concerning my marriage.

Today, I/we have a successful marriage.

Today, our marriage is free from infidelity, lack, disrespect, etc.

Today, I/we believe that we will have children.

Today, I/we believe that we will have enough finances to purchase what we desire.

Today, I/we will communicate better.

Today, I will see my mate as You see them.

Today, I/we pray for the success of our marriage and call it victory.

Today, we will have FAVOR with all men.

Today, doors will open for us.

Today we will.............(Add your need/desire)

We see our marriage as You see it. Our marriage is whole, victorious, not self-serving but giving.

We will set a good example for our children and family. Thank You, Father, for VICTORY. In Jesus Name AMEN!!!'

About the Authors

Nyjha Andrews

As the founder of NAM (Nyjha Andrews Ministries), Nyjha is passionate about awakening, discipling, and empowering individuals to reign in their God-given purpose. The ministry is deeply rooted in her personal journey of faith and divine encounters, driving a mission to transform lives through the power and love of Jesus Christ. Nyjha currently resides in the DFW area. She is a devoted wife to Charan Andrews and a mother of four beautiful children. With a strong background in education, Nyjha serves as an Assistant Principal and holds both a bachelor's degree in Business and a master's degree in

Education.

Vater Williams

CEO of Building the Wasted Places

Ministries Vater Williams has operated in multiple areas of ministries. 25 plus years ago, the Holy Spirit said, "When I wake you at night, get up and pray." From that time until now, intercession has been an active part of her life. She has spent the last 25+ years in Human Resources, focusing on Marketplace Ministry and connecting to God's Leaders in the corporate space. Vater is married to Gregory Williams, and they have a blended family of 6 kids, 5 grandkids, 1 great granddaughter and lives in the DFW area.

Contact us at: <u>Mendingthevow@gmail.com</u>

www.ingramcontent.com/pod-product-compliance
Lightning Source LLC
Chambersburg PA
CBHW040200160726
48006CB00014B/1832